The Taste of the Earth

THE TASTE

OF THE

EARTH

poems

Hedy Habra

Press 53
Winston-Salem

Press 53, LLC
PO Box 30314
Winston-Salem, NC 27130

First Edition

Silver Concho Poetry Series
edited by Pamela Uschuk and William Pitt Root

Library of Congress Control Number
2019943004

Printed on acid-free paper
ISBN 978-1-950413-09-6

To Nabil, for his loving support

The author thanks the editors of the following publications where these poems appeared, sometimes in a slightly different version:

ArLiJo 54: Arlington Literary Journal, "Jacaranda"
The Bitter Oleander, "The Abandoned Fountain"
Blue Heron Review, "The House of Happiness"
Blue Lyra Review, "The Dust of Legends"
Cimarron Review, "Topography"
Fifth Wednesday Journal, "I Came to Be Called the Damascene Rose," "The House in Aleppo That I Will Never Get to See," "What Every Blossom Hides"
Gargoyle, "Vanishing Point"
Ghost Town, "Hall of Mirrors," "Stepping into Mirrors"
Jabberwock, "The Broken Jug"
The Kerf, "No Man's Land"
Life and Legends, "The Colors of Dawn"
Live Encounters Magazine, "Defying the Blank Page," "Meditations Over the Eye of Horus-Sight," "Phoenicians Once Sailed from These Shores"
MAYDAY, "Tesserae"
Mizna Literary Journal, "The Abandoned Stone House in Damascus," "I'd Like to Write a Song of Freedom," "Close-Up on Tahrir Square," "Recurrent Dream," "Signs of Spring, 2011" "To Amal," "Visiting the Generalife"
One, "The Green Line"
Peacock Journal, "Deeper Than Tattoo"
Pirene's Fountain, "Erasing the Memory of Fear" (formerly "Liberation Square"), "Close-Up on Tahrir Square," "Once Upon a Time, an Olive Tree," "What's in a Cup?"
Poetic Diversity The Litzine of Los Angeles, "Reading by Candlelight"
Sukoon Literary Journal, "After Twenty-Five Years," "The Hand of an Honest Man," "Eating Pizza in a Renovated Hammam in Granada," "The Lucky Ones," "The Map of Memory," "Meditations Over Phoenician Letters," "Song Rising from the Depth of Sorrow," "The Taste of the Earth"

ANTHOLOGIES

Aeolian Harp Series: Anthology of Poetry Folios, Vol3, "The Taste of the Earth," "Writing in Dust," "Deeper Than Tattoo"
Anima Methodi, "Riding the Winged Tricycle"
Carrying the Branch: Poets in Search of Peace, "The Green Line"
First Water, The Best of Pirene's Fountain Anthology, "Erasing the Memory of Fear" (formerly "Liberation Square")
Grit & Grace: A Woman Writing Anthology, "Reading by Candlelight"
Peacock Journal Anthology: Beauty First, "Deeper Than Tattoo"
Collateral Damage: A Pirene's Fountain Anthology, "No Man's Land," "To Amal"
Glass Lyre Press Anthology: Carrying the Branch: Poets in Search of Peace, "The Green Line"

Silk & Spice: A Pirene's Fountain Anthology, "The Abandoned House
   in Damascus," "Jacaranda"
Verse Daily, "To Amal"

CHAPBOOK
*Nazim Hikmet Fourth Annual International Poetry Festival Awards
   Winners: A Chapbook of Talks and Poetry*, "I Always Knew I Was a
   Sibyl at Heart," "Weaving and Unweaving," "Writing in Dust"

Contents

I

Topography

Sometimes I think my face is a map,
each line a faint record of hidden scars,
of what I've seen or felt. My skin retains
traces of every fleeting breeze, of drifting
snowflakes, remembers the warmth
of noonday sun, the salty trickle of sorrow
mixed with raindrops, and even the slightest
shiver, the music of light melting down my cheeks.

An imprint remains of the faces
whose gaze lingered over my face
with fingers on the tip of their words,
or outlined my features with fingers
weighed down with words. I often see
that other face beneath the one looking
at me in the mirror, swelling with recollections,
unraveling all my senses.

The Taste of the Earth

Two fawns cross the creek. One of them pauses, linked
to his mirror reflection by the tip of his tongue, parallel
worlds merge on the fault line of a folded image.

A musical phrase sticks to your skin, the wind espouses
ripples, liquid dunes lick the shoreline, give moisture to
wild brush, blown-over seeds and thoughts.

Iridescent hummingbirds hover over purple iris blooms.
The shore is faithful to the stream's first touch. Like first
love, it nourishes tendrils rising into a green flame,

never forgotten like the taste of the earth. A desert thirsts
for an oasis, a fawn melts into the music of a fable,
a gazelle, new memories map rhizomes twisting,

anchoring us farther with each shoot spreading from our
birthplace to everywhere we've lived, to where we live
now, and does it make a difference if the root remembers?

I Always Knew I Was a Sibyl at Heart

I have paid my dues and fought mood swings
before entering that stage of well-earned wisdom
preventing me from climbing over walls in midday,
pacing interminable labyrinthine pathways or drowning
in the deep wells of insomnia.

I've collected enough books to keep me company
till the day I die, stacked in double and triple rows,
in an arbitrary order they refute in unison. Each
volume stares at me with eyes shut, scrutinizes
my movements, tries to lure me into caressing
its spine, opening it like an *I Ching*.

Shouldn't I, on account of my years, be granted
the Sight, recognize the rhythm of unspoken speech
in the folds of each palm, read the veins of each leaf
blown by the wind? I could be scrying in the moonlight,
eyes wide open like a wise owl sensing the slightest
reflection on still water.

Hall of Mirrors

First, there's the mirror of memory: you only need
to refuel it with lies and illusions, project it onto a
screen, winding up sequences of animated scenes at will.

In the dormant well of memory
  you seek yourself and lose yourself,

sit for hours on the polished lip of the well as you
meditate over your lengthening shadow, perform a
makeover of your mind to erase the ravages of time:

a touch of blush over cheekbones blurs gravity lines,
tilts features upwards, and if this fails, a few hours
of sleep should put a glimmer in the eyes, redress

drooping eyelids, avoid the unsightly X-rays of your mortality.

Then comes the mirror of forgetfulness: swallowing bit
by bit your selective memory, stretching time and space,
a fluid mirror clouded with ripples, rippling memories

the elusive mirror in which
  you drown night after night

searching for answers to the same questions. You
wish to turn nightmares into paradise: sleep paralysis
overcomes you as past and future merge on their own

terms, choose their own colors, glide in swift motion,
deafening rhythmic steps resound in premonition,
emerge erratically from the recesses of your mind,

inaudible tunes fall, scatter like the last leaves of autumn.

Defying the Blank Page

They seem sketched at dawn with sepia colors: a herd of deer followed by a trembling fawn appears in the whitened landscape. Disoriented, they roam around unable to distinguish what was once inert or throbbing under the thick layers of immaculate snow. Head bent, they fumble, in search of a blade of grass, a twig or a dried leaf to munch on. They know they must keep digging deeper and deeper, farther and farther, until they stumble upon a forgotten nut or an acorn, the remainder of a bush, softened fallen bark still covered with moss, any meager sustenance to help resist the bitter cold. Are they even aware they instill hope in my daily struggle?

They gather at noon
warm a bed of fallen leaves
under the spruces

Writing in Dust

Let's weave braids of dust rich
with time's unspeakable
debris, broken voices, whispers,
dried tears, insects' wings.

Doesn't most of it come from
our discarded skin?

Or is it the residue of fleeting
breaths hidden in pillow edges
and seams, my kitten's fur,
conjuring my old cat's scent
alive in this impalpable,
minute form?

And is it true you can clone someone
with just one hair, one speck of flesh,
all of which hovers around you?

Some say don't clean too much,
a house full of dust is a sign
of laughter, of good times
spent forgetting how to clean.

Some say chasing spider webs
in every nook and corner isn't healthy
while unaware of those nesting
in one's mind.

Let's shake the dust in our heart
watch it fall like snow in a crystal globe,
paint open shutters, let the wind in

or think of what we might
write in our own dust
as on a sandy shore,
express the unthinkable,

unravel what informs that dust
let it settle at will
heavy as sand in an hourglass.

What Every Blossom Hides

The faceless woman wants to be incognito.
Or are her features erased with tears? She lies
under the tree, a mute witness to her half silences:

rising echoes trapped within the trunk, fading
as limbs twist in tortuous embraces, try to reach
the blue sky, away from original sounds

    each bud is a cry she has learned to withhold

She wishes for flowers to carry her words,
watches how petals blown by the wind form
a collage of repressed emotions. But who will

read the stained language of bleeding blossoms
losing their substance, dripping liquid words
heavy with memories of crushed limbs,

    of stones dismembered as walls crumble?

Only those who can read dreams embodied in signs,
decipher wrinkled scrolls, forgotten love letters
written on crumbling parchments, ashes of graffiti,

only those who once slept under these roofs,
had their hands tied, tongues severed by grief,
lost their shadows as they fell, unable to go on

    will know what every blossom says or refrains to say.

Once Upon a Time, an Olive Tree

My elders were chopped down and burned,
their roots too deep to uproot, their veins spread,

shoots spoke in tongues, mapping the field,
an invisible presence throbbing under the earth,

thirsting for each raindrop, remembering every bird's
trill and nest, the air redolent with blossoms,

the smell of grilled skewers, baking stones,
freshly roasted coffee, feet stomping the earth

with joy, a rhythm of life inscribed in every pore.
Will children ever know how much I miss their branches'

lacy shadow woven with stories and wisdom?

The Dust of Legends

Watch this dewdrop in suspension
        on the tip of a twig;
                see how its iridescence trembles
between leaving and staying,
        saying and holding back?
It seems to sink in its own reflections,
        the way we feel
                when we wonder if we've left
a furrow, or a trace of ourselves
        in someone else's thoughts?

And hasn't everything we dream,
        think or desire, always been there,
                hidden between the lines,
or in the stacks of photos, collected
        and never looked at again?
How can we revisit dreams, when dreams,
        kneaded with words
                petrified by indifference,
evaporate in wisps of smoke
        at the touch of a pen?

What of this rootlessness that settles
        when walls collapse
                into dust as we search
for new equations
        to rebuild our notions
of belonging, memory or desire?
        When we no longer take the time
                to listen to ourselves
or hear whatever things
        may have witnessed and stored deep inside?

How many grains of sand will the soles
        of our feet have touched
                between birth and death?
How many caresses
        can our body remember,

how many fingerprints
       would still be burning our skin?
              How much life can be recaptured
and projected
       on the screen of our mind?

And yet, we once stood clinging
       to one another, as though
              about to fall from a cliff;
your breath warming my neck,
       your body espoused mine
like folds of a custom-made garment.
       We had become that tree in my backyard,
two trunks merging like twisted limbs,
       silence shrouding us
              with the dust of legends.

The House of Happiness

I wanted to revisit the house of happiness
and found open doors and windows
a house where anyone can enter and I can't step out

I tried to dive into the swelling well of memories
slide between yellowed images
sample once more the bittersweet taste of farewell

I used to walk by jasmine hedges redolent
of passersby thread white buds
rolled around my wrists rippling over my chest

I wished to retrace forgotten steps steeped in oleander
but only see dried-up vines deserted
sidewalks where shadows sink in their own reflections

What's in a Cup?

To see the world in an upturned cup,
      and watch your whole life unfolding,
I will make you Turkish coffee.

      Let's drink it almost boiling, a ritual,
sip every drop like nectar, turn the cup over
      then leave it up to me to decipher

the coffee dregs' configurations.
      See, there is a tree firmly rooted,
twisting in pain as Dante's suicides, relentless

      beaks tearing its gnarled branches.
See these parallel lines? They are ways of escape
      from your torment, trips you took in dreams.

See how they rise in volutes of smoke, free of fear?
      See the fish flying in the air?
This is money you will cash soon, very soon.

      See these narrowing paths barred at the top?
Obstacles will slow you down, but good news
      defile, countless like a procession of ants.

      Now with eyes closed, conjure up
each image engraved in your cup
      as if it were precious crystal.

Eating Pizza in a Renovated Hammam in Granada

was the closest I'd ever get
to that sensuous space envisioned
by Gérôme & Ingres.

Sunrays filtered through
star-shaped skylights
cast geometric shadows
over the tables,
broken lines drifted
across the dark marble floor,
a floor where odalisques' bare
skin was revealed by
the artist's brush,
the way Gauguin
unclothed his *vahine*.

The furnace once used to heat
water was perfect for baking,
the owner said *¡A pedir de boca!*

I was told as a child
the real story
behind these arched doors,
how after their ablutions,
families rested over
carpet-covered benches,
drinking dark tea & sampling
the same pastries my Aunt Zekiye
brought yearly
in her luggage,
all the way from Damascus.

Private spaces where mothers
could find a bride for their sons
making sure their curves
weren't fake,
measuring the fullness
of their chest
& the width of their hips.

Visiting the Generalife

I linger along the rose orchard cooled by water fountains. A suspension of iridescent droplets rises and falls in splashing loops, trickles through inlaid channels. Here, air speaks with caressing syllables and fragrant language; each lemon tree heavy with golden globes, its crisp shiny leaf ready to break under my fingers' slightest touch, oozes essential oils. Each rose speaks of the harvest of rose petals and orange blossoms my mother distilled in alembics in the vast white-tiled bathroom, the transparent essence imprisoned in a row of bottles stored in the *sandara*, that secret room above the kitchen, hosting a microcosm of flavors gathered from faraway plantations and mountain slopes.

Boabdil's heart shrunk
eyes fixed at the Alhambra
a fragile star falls

Tesserae

When I close my eyes
      I see the child in me
hug the hour hand
      licked by the flame
of memory emerging
      in stark darkness

a faint light filters
      through cracks
a half-open door
      frames a shadow
tiptoeing to make
      the moment endure

some nights fired
      tesserae reassemble
the father who left too soon
      guides the child's
first steps holds the tiny hand
      over the ruled page

II

Meditations Over Phoenician Letters

Words were born at the dawn of time in Jbeil, Byblos, the oldest inhabited city in the world. Symbols appeared inscribed over the skin of goats and sheep, bearing visual messages that sailed from shore to shore undergoing an alchemical transformation, still echoing the same sounds in other tongues.

I.

Aleph for ox marking furrows in parallel lines, erect like that first letter initiating the article, *al* for *aleph*, the one and only of its kind, encompassing all meanings.

Beth, *bayt* for house as bosom, womb, *al bayt*, where families gather around the homemade meal cooked over a hearth, often bearing a burning dot under the cast iron tray.

Gimel for camel, ships of the desert, *al gamal*, battling dunes as waves head bent, back curved under chests filled with gold and spices, eyelids heavy with the secrets of Timbuktu.

Daleth for door, half open *dal* hospitality leading to *al dar*, a heart with open valves to transfuse friendship, erase boundaries, a steaming stew's scent welcoming you in.

He for a window's delicately laced wood, musharabiyehs filtering the sun, letting the wind in, *al hawa'* from each cardinal point, allowing *al hawa*'s ethereal love to hover along the walls.

II.

Waw for hook uniting letters forming words or setting the tone as a vowel, mouth in awe for wow, *al waw*, asking for more, doubled in the depths of *noor*, the light, and *osfoor*, the bird.

Heth for stones erected for lamentations, *al hayt*, separation, veiled with graffiti, muralist paintings, a wall to be destroyed, leaving only its pillars for memory.

Yodh for *yad*, a hand for lovers hand in hand, for building, cooking, painting, hand shaken in a peace agreement, asking for a daughter's hand, granting her hand. Would a girl's hand always belong to a man?

Kaph for palm, applause, *al kaph*, life lines filled with expectations, holding a wealth of cherries or raspberries, a measure for caresses, a palm filled with water to quench your thirst.

Lamedh, *lam*, for unattainable desire, frustrated springs, a liquid lambda, flowing stream filled with lost opportunities, forgetfulness, yearning to settle down on the shores of earthly hope.

III.

Mem, the letter *mim,* conjuring water: *al may'* droplets of dew, ripples or waves, ambrosia, gold nuggets buried in deep wells for the desert voyager, Andalusian fountains whose crystalline notes echo *al oud.*

Nun for the letter *nun,* for the tail of *al thu'ban,* curling up into itself, an uroborus, *nun,* marked at times with a dot for its piercing eye, the end and the beginning, a restless eel leaping out in foaming spirals.

Aiyn for eye, a lidless eye lined with Kohl, right inside Fatima's palm, a blue amulet conjuring *al ayn,* the evil eye, the Sight that opens the gilded gates of consciousness.

Pe or feh, *al fam* for mouth lined with carmine lips to surround love words, the kiss, the silence, the breath, opening and closing the door to the soul, the spirit of life or death.

Qoph, another sign for palm, yet closer to *al qird* for monkey: it once was a gird for three monkeys, *al qouroud,* spinning the wheel of fortune, the one on top flaunts a fleeting crown, but his luck is changing, unless he'd master the wisdom to say nothing, see nothing, hear nothing.

IV.

Resh, for head, *al ra's,* harboring inner thoughts, true feelings under hats or veils, the mirror we wish to present to the world, the leader or dictator, the crowned hero or the beheaded.

Shin for tooth, *al senn,* losing one in a dream means the passing of a loved one, losing them all at once is the end of love. A tooth can be a sign of strength, a serpent's fang, or a way of identifying a skull.

Teth spins the thread of life around *al takht* for bed, and *al tamar* the palm tree, the fabric lovers' sheds are made of, its dancing fronds inspire tales that conjure the simoon, measure the inclination of the wind, drift into the unknown under sand storms.

Samekh for fish, silvery scales glittering in circles, *al samak,* intangible, mercurial, like words whispered in the dark, slippery oaths and good omens in dreams, harbingers of cornucopia when they rise from the bottom of your Turkish coffee dregs.

Zaiyn for a sword shaped as a sickle, a scimitar, *al zayn,* perfection, as the number seven and the mandala circle, infusing inner beauty and grace for *al zahra,* a white blossom delicate as jasmine, or *al zohoor,* an orange tree bursting with blooms.

III

Riding the Winged Tricycle

When Saturn's three crescent moons enter
their wild dance, I see myself riding
the winged tricycle of my youth towards
an open nave that grows into a caravel
flaunting my winged effigy on its prow,
a figurehead that appears as the centerpiece
of a gilded triptych while concentric dark
brushstrokes around my wide-open eyes

convert me into a revered icon, glowing
crescents hover above my head, halos
inscribed within the alignment of Orion's
three stars, ominous signs tell me that age
is but an illusion, that I can ride that small
bike, soar, heady with my childhood
dreams, dizzy with the illusion that past,
present and future come together at once.

Recurrent Dream

Anxiety erodes my sleep night after night
as memories and fantasies collide. Heartbeats
merge, projected onto a screen at full speed,
till my heart loses its elasticity, unable to
bounce back: a dull horizon appears flattening
waves and desert dunes, a serene landscape
without ups and downs nor a change of seasons,
till the screen erupts ablaze, we enter a country

torn by civil war, trapped in winding alleys
with checkpoints, danger lurking in every
corner. I am back wherefrom I fled decades
ago, and now, I'm lost, dream after dream in
the wrong neighborhood: I can't ask for a ride
home, home is the enemy, can't find my way back
to safety. Desperate, I realize I am getting closer
to the straight line that accompanies silence.

No Man's Land

She was gathering thyme
on the winding hills
of South Lebanon

Two bullets
pinned her
to a thorny bush

Instead of wings
she had her harvest
of thyme.

Phoenicians Once Sailed from These Shores

Fishermen, shoulders bent,
set sail daily,
carrying baits,
oil lamps, a loaf of bread.
Theirs a biblical patience,
taking them farther
every day,
muscles tight, foreheads furrowing,
awaiting the secular miracle,
their nets deployed
in an ancestral garb,
flutter as a dancer's veil
enveloping the dense,
sterile Mediterranean waters,
scooping algae, residues, dead fish,
fugitive ripples.
They return home empty-handed,
later every time,
at dawn or dusk,
eyelids lowered,
disappearing under thick eyebrows,
their flattened nets
heavy with absence

To Amal

Because your name means hope

How can one think of better
days when streets
swarm
with armed men,
their uniforms
changing
with
the drift of war,
their faces the same,
their eyes, your son's eyes.

Amal, your name means hope,
yet years
go by, darkening
days with violent ink,
night's pulse
resounding
through splattered walls,
treacherous alleys.
And what's left
of your sweet name,
when deafened
by the sound of anger,

you dream you're lost in Beirut's
neighborhoods,
in search
of a way home
in the midst
of rubble,
faceless gunmen
check your ID
for a Cross or a Crescent,
at every intersection.

Unable to withhold your boy's finger
from the trigger,
you lie,
your nightmare, a faint echo
of raging battles.

The Green Line

Lebanon (1975-1990)

was drawn in front of my father-in-law's
        four-story building
on Rue de Damas
        Tarik El Sham the road to Damascus

We lived on the fourth floor
        were the first to leave
then the family on the second floor left

then the Melkite Orthodox Divorce Settlement
        Centre bronze plaque
was taken down
        from the first floor's door

Fighters placed heavy artillery on the terrace
        shooting aimlessly
across the Green Line

From the balcony my sister-in-law saw
a silhouette
        crossing Rue de Damas
from the St Joseph University

a red pool spread over the black asphalt
                of the infamous Green Line
snipers
        snipers
everywhere
        My father-in-law took his family and left

In Tucson, he raised canaries
        grew curly cucumber *mouloukhiyeh*
vines for stuffing mint & thyme

An old man with a weak heart
                he returned three times
to rebuild what was left

he kept returning with his music
and water pipe,
                recalling the days when
he'd just cross Rue de Damas

        to play backgammon
at the café terraces

The Map of Memory

in the heart of Beirut

We used to tour
the serpentine Souk Ayass,
       the ways of the past throbbing
side by side
       with the latest in fashion.

      Over the shops
where damask and silk
       were sold,
where words of bargaining
        warmed the air,
where a cup of Turkish coffee greeted
       every passerby,

fleeting clouds pass
       oblivious of the bustle
& glances that filled its winding alleys.

      In the Martyrs' Square,
bullet holes scar bronze arms,
       pierce legs and chests,
speak of layers of bloodstains,

      claim the secular monument
witness to lives lost
       —with or without a cause,

over which the wings of desire
       haven't swept
          the dust of destruction,
over which the winds of hope
       have stopped flowing.

      Decades later,
I no longer find
       my bearings, highways crisscross
a city once mine
       in the map of memory.

      A needed erasure after fifteen
years of madness,

an amnesic reconstruction,
sweeping dreams from stones,
        removing scars from façades,
remodeling features,

        balconies laced with wrought iron,
        windows graced with a triple arch,
        doorways heavy with footsteps,

all long gone with the echo of voices.

After Twenty-Five Years

I came to Beirut to retrace my steps but its warmth enveloped me in its ample mantle through streets I didn't recognize. Mushrooming bridges and roads led me to an array of Phoenician wrought iron letters rising over the Corniche railings like triremes' masts. I caught glimpses of an old house's blue mandalun windows, its arcades vivid in my dreams with its twin sister's face disfigured by open wounds.

Here and there, a jogger runs along the Promenade. Steeped in lost footsteps, the water seems darker as though hiding painful memories. Only the vendor of crisp sesame breads makes me feel at home; with a smile, he fills my *kaak* with fragrant *zaatar*. We won't linger in a café to sense the sea's mist suffused with bitterness, hear the stories of the wind; instead we go to the new *Friday's*.

I wish I'd pace the streets to gather some crumbs of what I miss the most, the traces of a city hiding within a city hidden under my eyelids. This is not what the heart remembers, I say to myself until the jacaranda's blue light anchors me back, whispering, yes, it's here, deep inside, fluttering like a dove's wings.

Reading by Candlelight

Bent over the page, I watch the light of the candle cast fluid shadows,
the way the cypress pierces low clouds with its vertical green flame,
flaring will-o'-wisps spring from the spiral staircase of my
consciousness, ferns unfurl in slow motion, spread liquid color
at dawn as fronds fill spaces once covered with snow,
the hearth's fiery tongues my cat and I watch flicker all night long,
the blue flame rising when I'd flambé cognac over crêpes suzettes,
the flicker of a match lighting a cigarette,
the infamous flames of a pyre or an auto da fe in a central square,
the flame of a candle I read about, lighting Camoens' table,
his cat sitting on a pile of notes eyes gleaming at the waning wick,
the poet keeps writing in the dark under the light shed from the eyes
    of his cat,
the tall flames casting a shadow-show of a couple's encounter over
    the walls of a cave,
flames rising from Beirut at night, as we watched from the mountains
    during the civil war,
the flames of violence filtered by the TV screen, more virtual each day,
still color the news, images hiding the smell of blood and charred skin.

Vanishing Point

Under a dark moon that has decided to keep silent, I wander along the street of chance, staring at the vanishing point, uncertain of the odds of being, but with the certainty that it leads to the sea. I walk like an automaton among passersby, gliding as faceless pawns. A couple of black horses pound the pavement, wavering between going forward or backward.

I wonder what lies for me at the end of this road lined with lamplights and palm trees. Fan-leaved branches stretch, unfolding an animated deck of cards turning into murals that grow in size. Shuffled and reshuffled at each step, some cards flip into a hall of mirrors in which I lose myself in my own reflections, as though in an old photo album where the faces of those now buried are fading.

> *we're crossing the bridge of death to leave behind*
> *the madness ... black sacks stained*
> *with blood ... stillness ... snipers ...*
> *a heart skips a beat.*

I walk faster, look sideways: some things are best forgotten. Let's fold the night into light. I pass a couple of young men who seem to get closer to me, then recede and peel off the murals, disintegrate like antique parchments at the sight of an imposing woman in Tyrian purple, a younger version of my mother who takes me by the hand and whispers in my ear: *There isn't a minute to lose.*

Weaving and Unweaving

I used to marvel at my mother's readiness
                    to unravel a sweater
          or unstitch

her needlepoint
          at the slightest error. Eyes fixed
                              over colored wool or silk
                    sliding through needles,

her racing fingers
                    fiddled in silence,
erasing long working hours.

          But why look at unweaving as erasure,

          or as Penelope's endless fight against time?

Isn't it rather a way to retrace one's steps?

                              Each gesture,
          an intimate journey into the weaver's
memory?

And isn't wisdom often equated
          with weaving and unweaving?

                    I think of the backwards movement
of the needle,
          unstitching every design,
                    yarn by yarn
                              as one erases a word,
                    letter by letter.

Each stitch removed leaves an imprint
                    on the fabric or loom a gaping space
          like footsteps,

          the way the tip of a pencil
                              scars paper fibers,

its invisible indentations
          only revealed by a brush of charcoal dust.

A careful erasure revisits the pattern. The image

       vanishes, not the roads that led to it,
          like a text whose lines haunt you

as you discard them one by one.

       A constant wavering between
          remembering and forgetting,
telling and retelling.

Deeper Than Tattoo

What is most deep is the skin.
—Paul Valery

Japanese *Kintsukuroi* fills
cracks with gold or silver,
its filigree tells the true story,
the way scars map our skin
and heart.

Shouldn't we unravel the plot
behind each hurt, unearth
however few gilded threads
remain?

Take that line on my right knee,
scenes unfold: back in grad
school, about to turn in an essay,
unable to get up,

crutches, hot baths, seventeen
unplanned stitches, my aged
mother up and down the stairs,
ice packs instantly

melting. Decades later, when
I count the glistening marks
laddered on my skin, I can still
see her entering

the room holding a wooden
tray with chicken soup and
toasted pita triangles spread
with labneh cheese.

Jacaranda

*Voy a construir una ventana en medio
de la calle para no sentirme solo.*
—Miguel Ángel Zapata

The poet would like to build a window in the middle of the
street so that he won't feel lonely. I also want to build a window
in the middle of the street, plant a jacaranda and then wake up
at the trills of the songbirds nested in its branches. I will drink
my morning coffee seated on the ground carpeted with the
purple petals of my youth and every night feel its foliage tremble
under the faraway breeze that blows in Beirut along the
Corniche, bringing a mist of fragrant echoes through half-open
shutters. Night is woven with the flutter of wings.

Windblown words travel
through thought's countless corridors
turn daydreams ablaze

The Burma Pearl

In my chest there is a dot that is a hole where I could hear my heartbeat as I stepped into the Burma store while you picked a pearl pendant just for me. That morning, dew was barely brushing the petals of the budding spring. I handed you my gold medal carved with the crowned Virgin and child, my grandmother's gift at my baptism.

I still have the oval-shaped pearl in my jewelry box; it has escaped looting, known so many homes in different latitudes and languages. It has never touched my skin since but remains filled with words said and unsaid, suffused within the music of a light that once ran over my cheeks.

Cicadas sing songs
hum a threnody for life
empty shells over bark

IV

Meditations Over the Eye of Horus

In Ancient Egypt, the Eye of Horus came to be known as
Wadjet, the most powerful of protective amulets made of gold,
silver, lapis, wood, porcelain and carnelian. The Wadjet's six parts
represented the shattering of Horus' eye and was associated with
one of the six senses as a specific fraction.

1. Smell = 1/2

Shem شَمّ

   This part of the Wadjet points to the nose and looks
like the nose.

I can still see the henna trees, awaiting like guardians by the
two pillars at the entrance of our home in Heliopolis. At night,
the creamy blossoms released their pent-up fragrance,
enveloping us in its mantle, guiding us in the darkness while
the *bawwab*, our janitor, slept in his narrow room under the
staircase, as though inside a pyramid. In the *Song of Songs*,
the Beloved compared Solomon to a cluster of henna blossoms,
his cheeks were beds of spices: he was a bundle of myrrh resting
between her breasts.

the moonflower blooms
only in total darkness
all eyes wide-open

My friend Mona would bring to class her boyfriend's handkerchief soaked in Old Spice. *Shem,* the deferred touch of a lover's approach. Or else, how could the pungent smell of a coat hanging on a hook, reeking of frying emanations, cause a body to ache with longing? And wasn't it during his Egyptian campaign that Napoleon wrote to Josephine, begging her not to bathe as he was on his way? Have we lost the animal? My cat sniffs dirty socks and underwear mouth agape with a mesmerized stare. I knew each of my babies' smell.

The skin remembers
the scent of essential oils
an invisible presence

◁ *Shem el Nessim,* the 'smell the Zephyr' spring festival originates in the pharaonic feast of 'Shamo,' or 'renewal of life.' It became the Coptic *'shem'* and coincides with Easter. How can one *shem* the breeze and resist the fetid scent of *fiseekh,* the inescapable salted fish placed in picnic baskets alongside green onions and hardboiled colored eggs? We always skipped the *fiseekh* part and started the day at the zoo. We'd get brown bags filled with dense paper balls tied with a wire. I can see us blow inside our fist before hitting the ground with tiny firecrackers. They made startling sounds and released a distinctive whiff . . . unaware of what would come generations later, explosions digging holes in the asphalt.

mimosa's pollen
nakha hanging in dense air
jasmine necklaces

Bakhoor, incense swirls rising in sign language to ward off the evil eye. Ancient Egyptians burned incense daily, a different bouquet for each magical spell or incantation. In funerary rites the soul of the deceased ascended to heaven by means of that ritual smoke thought to be the sweat of gods. And isn't there godliness in the tree's offerings, when one thinks of the pain inflicted to the bark's skin, each incision exuding a pearl-shaped tear? My *dada*, Mariam, loaded a brass pot, *mabkhara*, with coals and resins: she mumbled prayers and litanies, making circular movements in every room, lingering in the hallway under Mary's Greek icon lit by an oil lamp.

volutes of blue smoke
featherlike fingers disperse
ascending spirals

the smell of ambergris, myrrh and musk embedded in crypts,
                    funerary and alabaster vials
the smell of blown up churches and altars filling interstices
                    and crevices, impregnating every pore
the smell of sandalwood and frankincense saturating icons
                    for centuries with the smell of holiness
the smell of gunpowder fueling anger in Tahrir Square as
                    faces are faced with indifference
the smell of lentil soup with toasted cumin served to crowds
                    to wet their heart with a comforting aroma
the smell of crushed hopes melting into soot and decay
                    as darker shadows rise tainted with indifference
the smell of bodies packed against one another for weeks,
                    sweat speaking of bonding and merging goals
the smell of honeysuckle mingled with wafts of golden mimosa
                    when Heliopolis was still a model garden city
the smell of molecules of tear gas in suspension in the air
                    as rioting and chaos takes over chanting
the smell of attritive desolation rising from mote to mote
                    still present in the vacated and cordoned off square

2. Sight = 1/4

●

Basar بَصَر

> *This is the pupil of the Wadjet. It represents seeing or the sensation of light.*

In the nobleman Pashedu's tomb, the Wadjet is endowed with a hand holding a pot with flaming tapers. A god's eye bearing light guiding the hand as it carves and paints symbols on the vault's walls, lush everyday scenes to carry along into the afterlife. In Heliopolis, our house was wallpapered with my mother's oils: windows as thresholds, inviting me to step inside, near the girl seated in a boat, a young man eating her up with his eyes under the elderly fisherman's frown, or follow the couple watching the sunset from a terrace. Their silent message reached me deeper, year after year. The Book of the Dead spells on papyri or over murals ensured the path to eternal life. And aren't churches open books covered with sacred eyes staring at the faithful, piercing their hearts with invisible arrows? And don't colors and figures speak in tongues like Dante's *visibile parlare*, the bas-reliefs paving the way to expiation in his *Purgatorio*?

In mirrors I drown
find myself time after time
eyes lined with lapis

● Horus's lunar eye extends a hand, linking sight with touch. The Wadjet in midst of a palm wards the evil eye. Fatima's palm or *Khamsa* shows a finger for each of the five senses. Can we ever separate senses? *Kharaza zarka*, the tiny turquoise stone or blue-beaded eye we pin on cribs and babies' clothes alongside medals of the Madonna. Would a charm deflect malevolent looks? And does fear make things happen? *Lamh*, a quick glance or *albasar*, a flash of lightning, all wound in saccades like love at first sight: *nazra, summa ebtesama, summa algharam,* a look, then a smile, then passion. I see my mother's look in my own eyes, her sight and dreams passed on to me through her art before clouds covered her macula. I visit museums with her ghost by my side. She holds my brush when I paint what she will never see. I brought back from Spain a porcelain tile stamped with Francisco de Icaza's verses:

Dale limosna, mujer,
que no hay en la vida nada
como la pena de ser
ciego en Granada

Give him alms, woman
for there is nothing in life
like the pain of being
blind in Granada

Blind seers and poets had inner sight. All knew the importance of closing one's eyes to the world around us and entering another. When snatched from a dream, I hang on to fragments as brittle as old papyri that disappear leaving my chest an open wound. Can one conjure up a dream night after night with its final image? Ancient Egyptians understood that dreams open our eyes to gods' warnings and prophecies. Priests burned incense, chanting around a coffin sealed with wax in which a man was enclosed, before recording his near-death visions. It takes a lifetime to find an alphabet to weave the shreds of images projected onto the screen of our waking mind into a legible map that reveals our own features.

Broken mirrors shine
in memory's dark hallways
each a slivered moon

the sight of Poinciana's lush flames, their yellow
            stamen in flight
the sight of the Nile glittering in the felucca's wake
            under the moonlight
the sight of the woman's blue bra uncovered
            as she was beaten in Tahrir Square
the sight of pink and white oleander, our mothers'
            warning us of its blinding sap
the sight of Verdi's Aida's world premiere at the Cairo
            Khedivial Opera in 1871
the sight of the Cairo Royal Opera burning
            to the ground in 1971
the sight of Anubis weighing the heart of the deceased
            against the white feather of Ma'at
the sight of the gilded *iconostasis* and Christ's stern look
            as he raises his hand in blessing
the sight of the blue lotus rising each dawn from murky
            waters to reveal its golden heart
the sight of the *hudhud*, the hooded hoopoe carrier of King

Solomon's message to Belkis
the sight of colorful woven canopies erected in the streets
for weddings and funerals

3. Thought = 1/8

Fakr فَكَّرَ

> *This part of the Wadjet represents thought, symbolized by the eyebrow.*

My mother's perfectly traced eyebrows punctuated her mute directives in a secret language that controlled our pulse. When she'd say *kalbi kash zay alzabiba*, you have shrunk my heart into a raisin, we feared the next step, that of erasure, with the sempiternal *dawwabti kalbi*, you have melted my heart, as sugar dissolves in water! Ancient Egyptians believed the heart to be the seat of consciousness and wisdom. At the final judgment, it was weighed against Ma'at's ostrich feather to allow the deceased to cross the pathway to the Field of Reeds. Is this wherefrom we get our sense of love in connection with the heart? Does a thought espouse the rhythm of a heartbeat? When we forgive, don't we feel our heart lighter, freed from the ballast of bitterness and resentment?

the wind sweeps the grass
all over the Nile Valley
flowers bend their necks

Senet, or the game of passing, led players through the ten regions of darkness before rising dawn, offering a glimpse of immortality. I was often on my father's lap as he faced his backgammon opponents at the Club. I still feel the throw of dice on the wooden board, sense his excitement with each pawn placed in my hand. Nefertari is portrayed playing senet solo in her sheer linen dress and gold bracelets. Was she conjuring fate or her inner self, bracelets clanking together with each casting of lapis and ebony sticks? Through sepia lenses, I watch my grandmother on her wheelchair, playing solitaire for hours. Was she weighing the odds of walking again, despite Lourdes and her daily Bible reading? Her ghost wrapped itself in an ink wash around my mother, guiding her hands as she aligned cards, time after time. Borges was haunted by an eternal chess game in which "God moves the player and he, the piece / What god behind God originates the scheme ... ?" "*Dios mueve al jugador, y éste, la pieza /¿Qué Dios detrás de Dios la trama empieza ... ?*"

I play solo on
the white page, languages mold
my thoughts and feelings

My father placed blessed medals in the foundations of our home, in Heliopolis. He made sure to add *kharaza zarka* in its four corners. Invisible blue eyes watched over our sleep but kept him safe only for a few years. Were they asleep when he was on his deathbed? Spells and amulets covered vaults and coffins to ensure Egyptians a safe crossing in their last voyage, oftentimes in couples. Beatrice guided Dante towards his *Paradiso*'s higher spheres within the folds of a rose of light. Will love keep hearts pure and light? In which sort of paradise did my parents reunite? Is illicit love a sacrilege in the hereafter? In Thebes, Hatchepsut designed a tunnel between her burial chamber and her advisor's Senenmut. With his name carved on her mortuary temple walls, was she hoping they'd enjoy together eternal breeze?

Liquid words swallowed
phantom limbs awaken lust
for a lost body

I've always found it strange that I'd still remember our phone number from half a century ago, when those from successive homes in Beirut, Baabdat, Athens, Brussels and Tucson, vanished... 6-3-8-6-9 flows in my mind like beads running from a broken necklace. This Heliopolis number and the one in Michigan where we've lived for decades wrap the circle: an ouroboros merging time and space within a house we didn't build but where we've planted so many seeds it has become our Field of Reeds.

Ashen flowers rise
out of memory's embers
echoing your voice

The memory of the only day it rained during recess
                 at the Mère de Dieu College in Cairo
The memory of a sparkle of hope in extinguished young
                 eyes, shut off for no reason
The memory of the washerwoman hanging sheets, the wind
                 shrouding her over rooftops
The memory of Hypatia of Alexandria teaching philosophy,
                 astronomy and sciences
The memory of the widow's tears clinging to her cheeks
                 like dew at dawn over leaves
The memory of Sister Emmanuelle's life among the *zabbaleen*,
                 Egypt's trash collectors
The memory of wanting to walk through fire and memory's
                 fire soaring as the Phoenix
The memory of the *khamsin* blowing hot, sandy air for fifty
                 days through closed shutters
The memory of my first Arabic poem about befriending a bird
                 osfoorati, osfoorati, teeri ilaya wa rafrafi,
                     ya salwati fi khalwati,
                 ruffle your wings and come soothe my loneliness
The memory of manuscripts and scrolls burned in the library
                 of Alexandria by Romans, Copts and Muslims

4. Hearing = 1/16

Sam' سَمِع

This part of the Wadjet is shaped like an arrow or a musical instrument. It points toward the ear.

Christos' Vespa roared in the neighborhood: the one and only mobile nurse in Heliopolis, no thighs kept secrets from this injection superhero. Case in hand, his jovial *Yassou, Kalimera, Kalispera, Kalinita* preceded rituals of gurgling enemas held up high by a helping hand. At times, he'd swirl a blue flame inside small glass cups he placed upside down over my mother's chubby back. Mounds of pink flesh rose like cup cakes popping when removed, releasing evil winds from her lungs. My first kiss at the movies: you whispered *s'agapo* in my ear. I had to wait for Rimbaud to realize words were palettes and sounds carried indelible images. Summer nights, we'd hear the soundtrack from the nearby Riviera open-air cinema late reruns. Emanations of jasmine and honeysuckle mixed with fragments of dialogues. Moonlight filtered through shutters would turn the ceiling into a live screen on which we'd stage our own script.

broken words shiver
a double flame undulates
in chiaroscuro

I see myself at six sipping lemon *granitas* with my grandmother at the Palmyra café. The organ grinder's small monkey danced to the tune in his red vest and tasseled fez. He collected piastres from a tin cup. I was sorry for his chain, but scared of his butt, an overripe tomato about to explode. Hard to believe monkeys were once revered and mummified. Thot, the lunar god of writing, was often represented as an ibis or a baboon. How much godliness was left in the zoo monkeys we loved to watch? Did their fixed stare conceal the lost cipher to a secret alphabet as they'd relentlessly crack peanuts? Sometime after his death, we brought down father's wind-up gramophone from the *sandara* attic. Did the dog think his master's voice was trapped inside the horn? Maurice Chevalier startled us with Valentine's *tout petits tétons*, her tiny tits, and Mistinguett shrieked, *il m'a vue nue, toute nue*! The image of a woman in distress caught under the shower merged with my mother's oil of a nymph by a stream, waist loosely covered by a transparent veil. In ancient festivals, women danced for the goddess Hathor in diaphanous gowns or barely girded their waist with a loose belt.

Body sways lips sing
holy music for Hathor
sistrum strikes high notes

Priests touched the mummy's lips during the Opening of the Mouth Ceremony. In turn, the deceased could utter spells to regain power. We'd learn poems by heart *zay el bulbul*, as a nightingale. The *hakawatis* strung stories hours long in cafes in midst of shishas' whirling volutes of smoke. Tellers of lies that became truths like the making of history. Did Sheherezade's grain of voice entrance Shehrayar? Cleopatra must have had a velvety voice in each and every language for *her tongue was an instrument of many strings,* or so says Plutarch. Do mute voices hover over burial sites? Ask the 500,000 who inhabit Cairo's mausoleums. Are voices absorbed through kissing? Isn't lovemaking an opening of the mouth ritual to make a lover's voice endure? Your laughter still rings in my dreams. Through thick walls Layla could still hear her estranged Qays, or Majnun~the madman, reciting love poems in the desert. With eyes closed, she'd see him mark his longing with a stick on the sand's skin. Each verse enfolding the letters of her name, L-a-y-l-a~n-i-g-h-t.

Orpheus' head and lyre
floated on the river still
singing mournful songs.

The sound of finger cymbals clanging by vendors selling
      erk souss, licorice juice
The sound of Gregorian, Byzantine, Armenian, Aramean,
      Coptic and vernacular chants
The sound of harps, lyres, nays, qanuns, ouds, resounding
      in dream's endless corridors
The sound of the plaintive call of the muezzin at dawn
      when the world is silent
The sound of the swelling sepia waves lapping all night long
      in an abalone shell
The sound of deafening rain falling over memories lying
      in a boat drifting in high sea
The sound of dove wings whipping the wind over rooftops
      in the early evening

The sound of fragmented phone conversations punctuated
by islets of silence
The sound of words unsaid crowding one's mind, growing
louder year after year
The sound of Tahtib drums backing men's ancient stick
street dance, *ra's el assaya*

5. Taste = 1/32

Dhawq ذَوْق

This part of the Wadjet represents wheat or grain sprouting, blown by the wind; its curved tail symbolizes a falcon's feather.

Of all seven churches we visited on Holy Thursday in Heliopolis, the most lighted one was Notre Dame of Fatima. I'd kneel by the rod iron votive candle stand and watch the burning wick melt wax into stalactites. I'd gather the candle's soft edges to chew as prayers rose along the flame in furtive blue veils. Was that warmth a sort of spiritual nourishment? What if the absence of taste was the silence of taste, a denial of pleasure despite the taste of stealth, or a yearning for the sliver of moon we place on our tongue? Hasn't every pleasure always been there, hidden under our taste buds? Isn't age supposed to dull our senses, the way we forget the features of loved ones, their faces losing their contours along with the fading memory of a feeling or frisson?

Each recovered taste
opens a liminal space
filled with stills and scenes

Dhuq! Dhuqi! We were always summoned to taste! A word as a gateway to a tapestry of flavors we had to experience bite by bite. Spices can divide or separate. My nonna's shadow still wheels its way into my kitchen to supervise the right seasoning! Her final decree was punctuated by an orgasmic *Ya omri. . .* My life. . . head tilted, eyes disappearing under eyelids the way the diva Umm Kulthum swooned while she wailed her desperate *Enta omri*! You are my life! Many years later our pharmacology professor would face us with the same enraptured look after writing double-bind formulae on the board. Smoothing powders and unguents with pestle and mortars seemed a natural extension of grinding toasted coriander and cumin seeds with garlic and herbs. We learned to recognize dozens of white medicinal powders: we'd rub a small amount between thumb and index finger to sense its particle size, squeeze its sliding crystals or feel its impalpable fineness. But only one lick alerted the papillae.

Ancestral gestures
engraved over temple walls
etched inside our skin

Taste grounds us to the earth; it also involves touch and smell. And how can we separate it from sight or silent speech? Words and tastes are like grains of sand that form and gather, melt and solidify to form the most unexpected natural or man-made monuments. None of these grains is discardable, each lends itself to a particular texture, color or shape. Dad always offered me a foaming glass of *asab*, freshly squeezed sugar cane, from street vendors in downtown Cairo. . . I would rather chew on the stalk's sweet fiber but he'd insist, *Dhuqi! Dhuqi!* Taste! Taste! He'd drink his with delight, wiping the foam from his thin mustache. Later when I first sampled beer, its foam would remind me of those days when he was still around. Tutankhamon ale was brewed based on sediments found in earthenware jugs. Was its taste ever close to the pharaoh's liquid gold? Workmen at the Pyramids of Giza were given beer three times a day. Some tastes remain unnamed, immured in silence.

Bare-chested women
mixed barley, honey and herbs
for fermentation

The taste of the earth getting stronger each day
            as uprooted veins bleed
The taste that drowns in time within a thousand
            and one acquired tastes
The taste of *eshta baladi,* the thick buffalo-milk
            cream we fought over
The taste that keeps eluding us before stamping
            our brain with colors
The taste sketched so many times it vanishes within
            the shadow of an outline
The taste of black and white mulberries we picked
            from the tallest branches
The taste you wear around your neck like an amulet
            sewn in different flavors
The taste that spends a lifetime trying to retrace its steps
            and relocate its origin

The taste of Alphonso mangoes served finely diced
                into green Coca Cola bottles
The taste of a deeply engrained hope constantly renewed,
                growing back like a lizard's tail
The taste of *dora*, the roasted corn the street vendor
                fanned over sparkling coals

6. Touch = 1/64

▌

Lams لَمَسَ

This part of the Wadjet represents planting a stick into the ground, and also a tear.

A stick or a stalk that will take root, *gezr,'* and grow within the fertile soil of childhood, bearing marks of my mother's hands over fabric, canvas, our forehead, of her fingers rolling and braiding glistening dough. Falling down the cheek, each root swells and sprouts, writes its ephemeral music over underground scores. A tear, *dam'* a measure of time elapsed, leaving invisible furrows in its passage, moistening roots' fingertips as they feel their way in the darkness through dream's labyrinths. And what of those unshed, trickling inside, unseen? Do they moisten the heart or fill it with bitterness? Ancient Egyptians believed the heart was the seat of thoughts and emotions. Too precious to be handled, or preserved in canopic jars, it remained latent in the mummified body, waiting to awaken the tears of things. Mother would raise her open hands and smile: *When I'm gone, you should embalm my hands!*

What's love if not eyes
at the fingertips sorting
wordless twisted knots

Nany's voice moved listeners till her late seventies. A singer of the god Amun-Re, her burial papyrus shows her in her prime holding her mouth and eyes in an open palm while Anubis weighs her heart against Ma'at's ostrich feather. At school, each weekly confession spilled words out of our mouth, a river of guilt carrying away intentions, omissions, even the slightest dream of hunger or thirst. We'd rise, lighter, mouth and eyes carefully weighted in our hand. A hand that only knows itself by touching another skin, the way the fluid layers of water shape our body's innermost interstices. Still breathing of Egypt's Coptic period, the Fayum funeral portraits' dark eyes touch us deeply. Painted on wood as to give a face to the mummy, we sense in their stare the fear of the liminal threshold and can even feel the warmth pearling at the corner of an eye. They see us watching them as they once faced the artist's premonitory gaze.

Rain dots pierce the pond
fallen leaves cover its scars
thunder roars through clouds

Our pen and brush impress paper with words and visions that in turn entrap us. The fabric of the paper conveys the feeling it once felt. Words have a life like seeds; they just have to fall in the proper soil to grow and multiply. "Poetry sows eyes in the pages sows words in the eyes," "*La poesía siembra ojos en las páginas siembra palabras en los ojos,*" said Octavio Paz. Handwriting conjures a face, each faded letter, a glance, a touch, even shattered words bring eroded memories to life. The god scribe Thot records with a stylus and a palette his wife Ma'at's final verdict, sealing with words the passage to the Field of Reeds. Didn't Paolo and Francesca fall prey to words conveying the deferred touch of mythical lovers? An illicit kiss once read, begot another! Yet Dante placed them together in the second circle of his *Inferno* as two doves moved by the wings of desire, the same whirlwind embracing them in unison in ways they don't even register as touch.

An unwanted touch
as hard to dispel as a
haunting sky of lead

The touch of the roots' knotted filaments we pull from
            the earth like varicose veins
The touch of my newborns' tender skin softer than rose
            petals against my chest
The touch of the *aldaba*, the carved doorknob we'd rub
            with copper paste
The touch of the dormant frog I found as I was digging
            to plant bulbs in the yard
The touch of the Nile mud under the potter's fingers
            spinning before espousing flames
The touch of a book's spine held gently like an open chest
            as we turn its pages
The touch of clean, crisp cotton sheets filled with Heliopolis
            sunshine on Friday evenings
The touch of our bare soles over the sand licked by the warm
            foaming tide in Alexandria

The touch of piano keys striking notes that make us shiver
and lower our eyelids
The touch of Soumass, the kitten I hid inside my coat during
the school bus ride home
The touch of Byssus, the sea silk harvested from shells spun
for pharaoh's golden robes

V

I'd Like to Write a Song of Freedom, 2011

The daily news defies me as does the almanac when
early signs of spring sprout, in Egypt & Lebanon,
budding with innocence, walls rise, crushing voices
with indifference. I'd like to write a song of freedom,

a Song of Songs merging the dialects of my youth
into one heart, and share the lush ruby red arils of
Phoenician apples. Syllables fall off the table, lie
formless all over the floor, powerless, unable to unite.

How could they concoct an elixir of hope when time
and again in the land of milk and honey fear settles
its motto in streets steeped in carmine ink where shades
wander, forever haunting the site of their bloodshed.

Unable to decipher the elusive pattern of unuttered
words cluttered between my temples, a heavy armor
pressed against my chest, I only feel the lift and pause
of the waves surrounding silence. Will I ever learn
the language of invisible scars tattooed all over my skin?

Erasing the Memory of Fear

In awe, I watch on my television screen
how Egyptians openly storm the streets,
walk in throngs, chant in unison their
will for change, crowding Tahrir Square.

I still remember my youth, under rigid,
military rule, when lips were sealed,
when every wall had ears, when every
corner café, every restaurant table,
remembered our conversations.

That was so long ago: we chose
to leave, hearts heavy with longing.
Others got used to the status quo.

From far away, I marvel at the power
of images, when throbbing hopes
brighten ebony eyes, raise flags,
press bodies against bodies hours long,
oblivious of hunger and discomfort.

No dissonant gestures break the ebb
and flow of their unified voice,
rhythmically shaking their reclaimed
mare nostrum.

A page has been turned. Men
and women want to write letters
of freedom on their children's
foreheads, one by one,
cover the walls of their dreams
with glistening graffiti and sparkles,
erasing the memory of fear.

Close-Up on Tahrir Square

Ramses II was the first king to sign a peace treaty
inscribed on a silver tablet and carved into the temple
walls in Karnak

A matronly woman with a black headscarf
kisses a young policeman with blue eyes.
When did she ever get so bold as to break
through the creaks of rigid ancestral walls,

allow her breath to reach the warmth of a man's
skin other than her husband or sons.
Stunned, he lets her hold his helmet-covered
head between her palm and lips, feels her

mouth sink into his cheek as in quicksand,
he dissolves as though sucked into her womb,
becomes a statue of salt, both hands

frozen around his raised rifle, and sees his reflection
in the sun, face framed with the colors of peace.
Both wonder if a lamb will ever lie by the side of a lion.

Signs of Spring

Sunshine fires flakes,
                crystalline needles,
        uncovers a glossy landscape of frozen dew drops
                steeling timid tendrils' first breath.
Bold hyacinths stick out
        jade periscopes
                in albescent wilderness. Even willows
        yellowing by now in Kalamazoo,
                remain invisible,
pigments hiding inside each pore, eyelids
        heavy under coats of dried ochre,
                a cloud of rust blurs bushes and brambles.
Oaks' broken limbs still hang,
                lassoed by last year's
        vines shooting tentacles
around warped branches
        awaiting makeup from mushrooming moss.
                Soon, chartreuse ink will unfurl,
                        twisting its woven net
        around dark distorted joints.

Elsewhere, all over Egypt,
        spring comes to *Umm al dunya,*
                the Mother of the world,
with thumping pace, feet roaring
                in crowded squares, streets
resonating with raucous sounds,
                        shaking deep-rooted fears.
        Veins fill with the sap of freedom,
voices burst in vibrant flags,
        each poem spins volutes
of hope in the air,
        words cling like vines,
coil over the tallest towers,
        each drop of blood
                consecrates the ground,
        but no one bends to see how tender blossoms swell,
no one marvels at the pink and white oleander,

        the lush crimson palette of bougainvilleas,
no one notices
        the way jasmine hedges infuse
the air, their sweet scent mixed with pungent
            wafts of honeysuckle,
     no one is soothed
        by the enveloping perfume of golden
mimosa pearls in bloom.

The Colors of Dawn

A pantoum for peace

Spring rain washes out ashes and winter fears
Doves dip their wings in the colors of dawn
Children gather fallen petals, feather and down
Let's weave a tapestry with a thousand petals!

Doves dip their wings in the colors of dawn
Cherry blossoms cover the veined branches
Let's weave a tapestry with a thousand petals
Invent a new alphabet to record our dreams!

Cherry blossoms cover the veined branches
Let's paint windows and doors on stonewalls
Invent a new alphabet to record our dreams
Fingers string beads carved out of olive pits!

Let's paint windows and doors on stonewalls
Hang rosaries on the highest limbs and towers
Fingers string beads carved out of olive pits
Small hands gather pebbles to erase borders!

Song Rising from the Depth of Sorrow!

A pantoum for hope

Seeds of hope are written in invisible ink
Underlying despair they fold seasons at will
Stop tears of blood and bodies from falling
Keep rubbing with pumice stone and read!

Underlying despair they fold seasons at will
You can turn moon into sun and sun into moon
Keep rubbing with pumice stone and read
The pool of blood grows larger than the shadow!

You can turn moon into sun and sun into moon
Bring to the surface secret and repressed longings
The pool of blood grows larger than the shadow
Look at the glittering pattern of underground veins!

Bring to the surface secret and repressed longings
Curl into the moment preceding the bird's song
Look at the glittering pattern of underground veins
Listen to the song rising from the depth of sorrow!

Stepping into Mirrors

Stepping into mirrors is diving in deep sea.
Would the sea withhold the memory of sunken
bodies, bodies of migrants hoping to reach the shore?

Would mirrors remember familiar faces first
thing in the morning, the startled look before
the reassuring makeup, the daily questioning?

Would mirrors record the roundness of breasts
and their gradual falling, observe how curves
rouse when rubbed with scented essential oils?

Would mirrors bring to life my mother's early
ritual, features clouded by Coty's Muguet des Bois
fluffy puff, carefully outlining lips and eyebrows?

Would shards of shattered mirrors stamp severed
limbs, blood-soaked shirts, dust-covered skin, serve as
fingerprints for not turning the page, or swerve after cleanup?

Would the reflection subside forever, leave an
imprint outside of our own mind, coded messages
for us to retrieve from the other side of the mirror?

Would the sea withhold the memory of sunken bodies,
bodies of migrants hoping against odds to reach the shore?
Stepping into mirrors is diving in deep sea.

The Abandoned Stone House in Damascus

Don't ask me what side I am with!
Don't ask me about the outcome!

They say rain won't wash the indelible blood splattered in the streets, the moans and cries of children resonate in my aching ears, filling each crack and corner of my heart. Will anyone open doors and windows wide, let the wind in to erase the bitter clouds of gunpowder? Faces smeared with dust and sweat all look alike, come and go as they please, their footsteps resonate in my temples as over worn out, stretched out drums. My walls yearn for the daily smell of freshly cut herbs, for the warmth of the hearth, the familiar sight of the iron pot hanging over glowing coals. Once, the simmering stew was singing with spices and children played under the shade of the olive tree. I can still hear their mother's humming while separating lentils from stone.

The Lucky Ones

Withhold the lingering scent of soil & flowers

Orphans play
   with a ball of rags
      by the makeshift shelter.
A palace in midst of dust and rubbles.

An elderly woman
      rearranges her head scarf
  as she speaks.
      Her callous fingers
braid the little girl's rebellious hair.

      Her name is Samia,
she never lets me
      comb her hair.
It hurts! Only *mama* knows how!

The woman throws
      a clean mat over
the rugged floor,
      centers a pot of rice,
parts bread loaves in equal shares.

      Tfaddalou,
she beckons, holding
      a tall glass of dark tea.
No one speaks. She worries.

At sunset, most children
      will lie down on their cots
eyes wide open
      all night long.

The House in Aleppo That I Would Never Get to See

My father's ancestral home haunted me for years
like the mirage of an oasis that kept receding in my mind

I've lived in this house through stories told
by my grandmothers in Heliopolis, and
yellowed photographs bearing handwritten
notes. A dream stored in a drawer: year
after year, whenever in Lebanon, we'd say,
next time, we'll make it to Aleppo!

I will never sit in the internal courtyard, by
the marble fountain inlaid with pink stone
and basalt, watch the rise and fall of its
refreshing ferns constantly humming as I
sip my Turkish coffee.

I will never walk over the intricate
geometric designs of the marble floor,
surrounded by climbing jasmine and
rose bushes, lending their pungent scent!

On sleepless nights, I'd visit the wood-paneled
rooms, stare at the wall cabinets' calligraphic
carvings, letters engraved in gold leaf arabesques,
opening up like petals, each telling a tale. . .

The story of the secret passage, leading
from the cave to the once imposing Citadel,
offering the possibility of an escape, or
reaching out for supplies, alleviating
the anxiety of living under constant threat.

The story of the cave's arched chambers, redolent
with ghost smells and fragrances, the large
earthenware jugs pregnant with wine, vinegar or
olive oil, the handmade laurel soap squares, stamped
with an olive tree and stored to age for months.

The story of laurel bar shavings melted for laundry
on the terrace, clothes hanging on ropes basking in
the sun, nearby the open-air stone oven for baking
flat bread, braided Easter brioche and pastry trays.

I think of the wind blowing through immaculate
sheets, shrouding faces, an omen of what was yet
to come, the heat of the oven increasing, increasing,
stone walls crumbling with louder, ever deafening
sounds, and wonder, where did the songbirds go?

The Broken Jug

Aftermath

My cracks won't hold
rainwater any longer.
I wish I could still soothe
sore palms and dry throats.

How I loved to be raised
up in the air over a tired face,
let a trickle pour from
the tiny spout near
the curvature of my neck,

watch it dribble down
the corner of a mouth,
chin and chest, refresh
the back of a hand,
fingers dirty with soil.

My terracotta mantle
kept water cool under
intense sunrays,
sweat beads glittered
on my porous skin.

I've developed an inner
sight from nights spent
in open air, my clay
pregnant with echoes
of pleas, of children
sobbing, grinding
their teeth as they sleep,

once filled with whiffs
of incense and burning
wicks, now, in deafening
silence, only dust coats
my scorched edges.

I Came to Be Known as the Damascene Rose

Our origin is shrouded with mystery: some say
we thrived in distant lands, but came to be known
as Rosa Damascena. The heady rich scent
of our rippled skirts once graced Syrian rooftops,
balconies, and roadsides, before the air reeked

with gunpowder. Dried up farmlands have swallowed
our shadows. We bear the heavy burden of fallen
bodies, young bodies wrapped hastily in white shrouds,
a sterile graveyard weighing over our own. An oasis
sung by poets, the Ghouta, is now barren, its trees

reduced to ashes. When mature fruits fell, their juices
sank in sacrifice into the soil's deepest layers.
Leaves followed the movements of the air,
the flight of sunrays veiling and unveiling every bloom.
Lying under the scorched earth, like Sleeping Beauty,

we have stopped counting, mourning this unending winter
of strife and destruction. And bear in mind that we still
feel the sunlight through fissures and cracks, find moisture
within our own veins, sense every frisson of the earth,
every drop of dew soothing our pain; some of us have

risen and circled around ruins. We know we will all
blossom again under the warm breath of our caretakers.
Their callused fingers will once again gently prune
our stems, removing each spotted leaf one by one,
guide our canes and shoots around poles and trellises.

The Abandoned Fountain

I wasn't always covered with dust and fallen leaves. Water's cooling ferns once ran over my marbled veins, opening up and closing like fans. I knew the language of each ripple and secrets rippled through my heart, sighs of joy or pain filled my dreams until the day I woke up in the midst of rubbles.

In the deserted courtyard, children came to wash their naked soles, bleeding from cracks like hardened cement, but I was too dry to soothe their wounds. No one cleans my mosaic tiles any longer, no one rubs my copper faucets, no one sits on the smooth edges that were my pride. At dusk, shadows without a head chase limbs searching for blind shadows.

I hear voices, fractured like shattered mirrors, each searching for an ear, unable to find a match, lost cries soar in dissonance, rise in volutes of pain, circle around broken bricks and stones, disappear through holes and crevices. I know a river of voices runs down the streets surrounded with indifference, endlessly swelling, sending ashen messages to the wind.

Notes

"Riding the Winged Tricycle" (p. 27) and "Recurrent Dream" (p. 28) follow the Anima Methodi form based on the Poetics of Mirroring.

Conceived by Desmond Kon Zhicheng-Mingdé and Eric Tinsay Valles, the anima methodi is a 16-lined poem, comprising two stanzas of eight lines each. The structure has been quaintly called the twofold binate octave. Two words or phrases are repeated anywhere within the first binate octave, and the same mirroring effect (with the same or different pair of texts) is done for the second binate octave. There remains continuity across both stanzas, with the last line of the first stanza moving seamlessly— across the stanza break as dovetail—into the first line of the second stanza. The stanza break may also locate the poem's volta, as with the sonnet, for which, according to Phillis Levin, "the volta is the seat of its soul."

Artworks used as inspiration for the following ekphrastic poems:

"What Every Blossom Hides" (p. 9), *Girl with Magnolias* by Hanna Ilczyszyn
"Vanishing Point" (p. 37), *Surreal Board Games* by Juanita Guccione

HEDY HABRA was born in Egypt and is of Lebanese origin. She has authored *Under Brushstrokes*, finalist for the 2015 USA Best Book Award and the International Book Award for Poetry, and *Tea in Heliopolis*, winner of the 2014 USA Best Book Award and finalist for the International Book Award for Poetry. Her story collection, *Flying Carpets*, won the 2013 Arab American National Book Award's Honorable Mention and was finalist for the Eric Hoffer Award and the USA Best Book Award. Her book of literary criticism, *Mundos alternos y artísticos en Vargas Llosa* (2012), explores the visual and interartistic elements in the Peruvian Nobel's fiction. Habra holds a B.S. in Pharmacy. She earned an M.A. and an M.F.A. in English and an M.A. and Ph.D. in Spanish literature, all from Western Michigan University where she has been teaching. A recipient of the Nazim Hikmet Poetry Award, she won Honorable Mention from *Tiferet* and was finalist for *Nimrod*'s Pablo Neruda Award. A fourteen-time nominee for the Pushcart Prize and Best of the net, her multilingual work appears in numerous journals and anthologies, including *The Bitter Oleander, Cimarron Review, Connotation Press, Cutthroat, Diode, Drunken Boat, Fifth Wednesday Journal, Gargoyle, Letras Femeninas, Mizna, New York Quarterly, Nimrod, Poet Lore, Pirene's Fountain, Solstice, Valparaiso Poetry Review, Verse Daily* and *World Literature Today*. Her website is HedyHabra.com